The Delicious Doodles Collection

Shades of Greyscale

by Teri Sherman

ISBN-13: 978-1976524639
ISBN-10: 1976524636

THIS BOOK
BELONGS TO:

© 2017 Teri Sherman
AFRICAN WILD DOG
© 2017 Teri Sherman

© 2017 Teri Sherman

Big Horn Sheep

© 2017 Teri Sherman

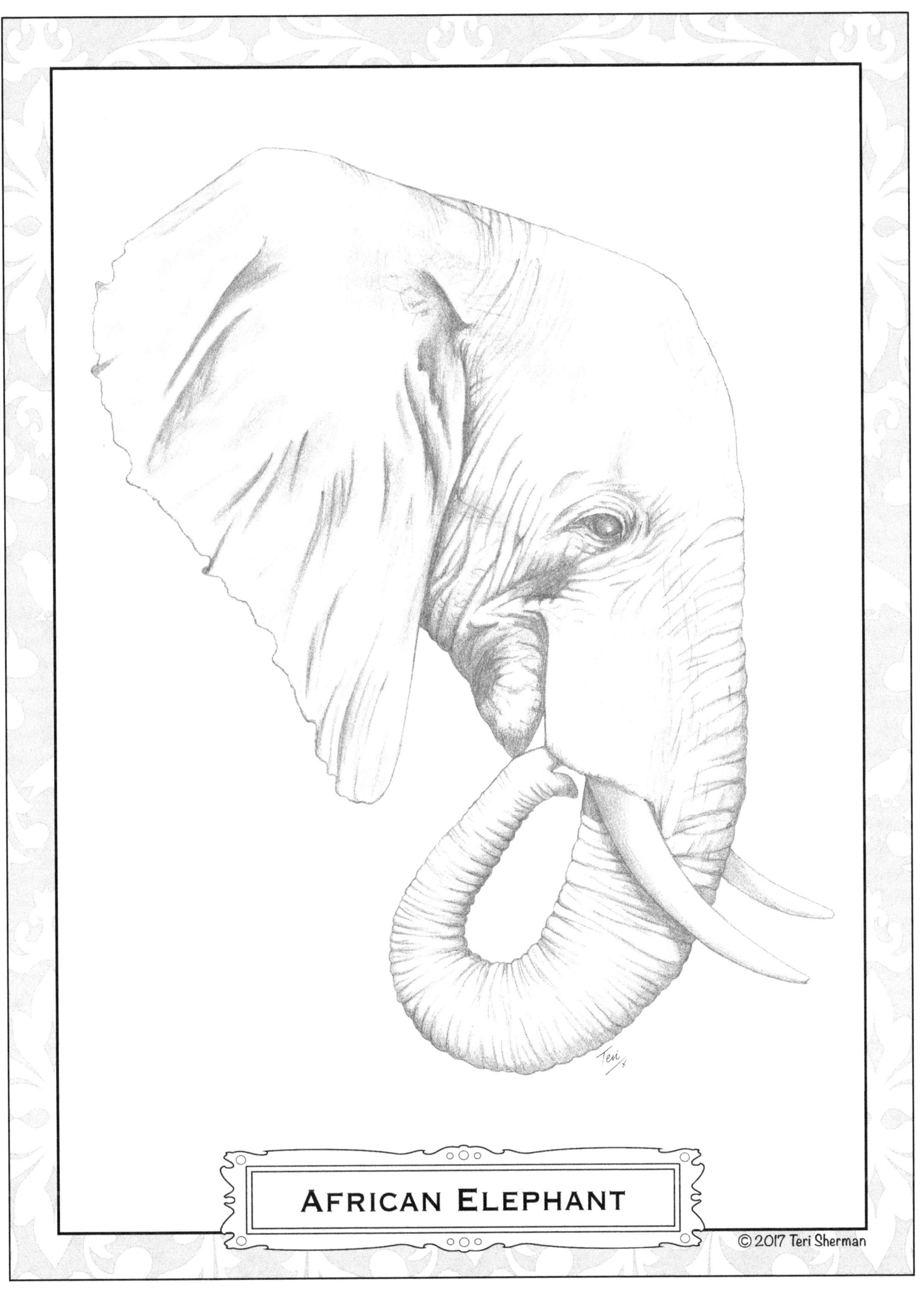

AFRICAN ELEPHANT

© 2017 Teri Sherman

Bactrian Camel

CARACAL

© 2017 Teri Sherman

GIANT ELAND

© 2017 Teri Sherman

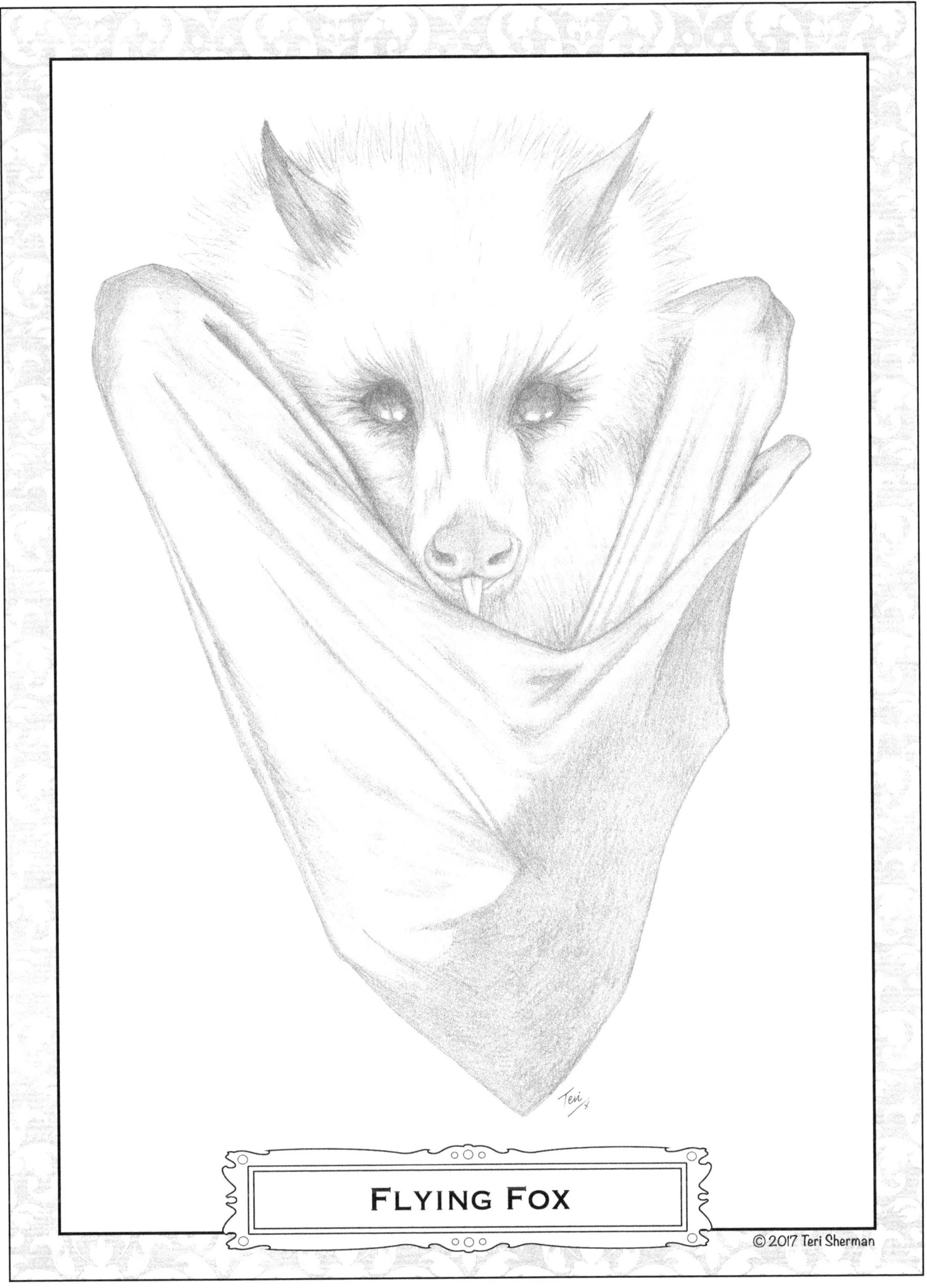

Flying Fox

© 2017 Teri Sherman

Gorilla

© 2017 Teri Sherman

HARE, OR JACK RABBIT

LEMUR

© 2017 Teri Sherman

Marmot

Okapi

ORANGUTAN

SNOW LEOPARD

WALLABY

Water Buffalo

WARTHOG

Zebra

© 2017 Teri Sherman

About the Artist

Artist, wife, mother of three, pet sitter, neglectful housewife, fair weather gardener.....

Teri Sherman has illustrated, crafted and coloured countless projects throughout her years.

Residing in a semi-rural village in Scotland she uses her artistic abilities to create colouring books and digital stamps.

Following the success of her first **Delicious Doodles Collection**, Teri has now created this beautiful new assortment 'Shades of Greyscale' for all the family to enjoy!

More Titles by Teri Sherman

Delicious Doodles Collection, Book One - Feminine
Beautiful collection of Feminine illustrations from the Delicious Doodles store

Delicious Doodles Collection, Book Two - Flowers and Animals
Gorgeous collection of Flowers and Animals in line art and grayscale from the Delicious Doodles store

Delicious Doodles Collection, Book Three - Myth and Magic
Fabulous Fairies, Magical Mermaids and other Mythical illustrations in line art and grayscale from the Delicious Doodles store

Delicious Doodles Collection, Book Four - Season's Greetings
A seasonal collection of Christmas and Winter illustrations in line art and grayscale from the Delicious Doodles store

Colouring Through The Year
Florals, Calendars, Festivals, Gods and Goddesses. This book is fun for all the family to enjoy!

Gothic Halloween
Teri's first venture into the world of colouring books gives you a myriad of Halloween style images, with some having a more gothic theme.

Dark Skies
This is a darker, more conceptual book filled with 'grayscale' (meaning already shaded) gods, goddesses and beasts born of celestial legend.

The Skullie Collection
Lots of Animal and Human Skull illustrations, with flowers and feathers and more!

GothArte Tenebris
More Skullie pics, with Gothic Style Illustrations too!

Connect with Teri
On Facebook, https://www.facebook.com/TeriShermanArtist
On Instagram, https://www.instagram.com/teridoodles
Etsy Shop, https://www.etsy.com/uk/shop/TeriShermanArtist